# OUR GOVERNMENT

# The President
## and the Executive Branch

**Bryon Giddens-White**

**Heinemann**
LIBRARY

Chicago, Illinois

Designed by David Poole and Calcium
Illustrations by Geoff Ward
Originated by P.T. Repro Multi Warna
Printed in China by WKT Company Limited

07 06 05
10 9 8 7 6 5 4 3 2 1

**Library of Congress Cataloging-in-Publication Data**
Giddens-White, Bryon.
  The president and the executive branch / Bryon Giddens-White.
      p. cm. -- (Our government)
  Includes bibliographical references and index.
  ISBN 1-4034-6601-7 (hc) -- ISBN 1-4034-6606-8 (pb)
  1.  Presidents--United States--Juvenile literature. 2.  Executive departments--United States--Juvenile literature.
I. Title: President and the executive branch. II. Title.
  JK517.G525 2006
  352.23'0973--dc22

                              2005008664


**Acknowledgments**
AP Wide World Photo pp. 8, 10 16 (Charles Tasnadi), 21 (Maxim Marmur), 24, 28 (J. Scott Applewhite); Corbis pp. 4 (Bettmann), 5 (Bettmann), 6 (Bettmann), 7 (Burstein Collection), 11 (Bettmann), 12 (Bettmann), 18 (Ken James), 20 (Brooks Craft), 22 (Burstein Collection), 26 (Saba/Najlah Feanny), 27 (Saba/Najlah Feanny); Social Security Administration p. 25; Getty Images pp. 1 (Taxi/Jerry Driendl), 29 (PhotoDisc/PhotoLink); Library of Congress p. 23; National Archives and Records Administration p. 19; U.S. Army p. 17 (Harry S. Truman Library).

Cover photograph of the White House reproduced with permission of Getty Images (Taxi/Jerry Driendl.)

Every effort has been made to contact copyright holders of any material reproduced in this book. Any omissions will be rectified in subsequent printings if notice is given to the publishers.

Special thanks to Gary Barr and Paula McClain for their help in the production of this book.

# Contents

Any words appearing in the text in bold, **like this**, are explained in the Glossary.

# The President Enforces the Law in Little Rock, Arkansas

During the 1950s, racial **segregation** was common in some areas of the United States, especially the South. Southern officials segregated, or separated, blacks by preventing them from going into white neighborhoods, businesses, and schools. In 1954, however, the U.S. **Supreme Court** declared the segregation of public schools **unconstitutional**. The court told public school officials that they must begin admitting all students, including blacks.

Some schools resisted the change—most famously Little Rock Central High School in Arkansas. At first, school officials in Arkansas cooperated with the court's decision. They made a plan to **integrate** Central High and chose nine black students from hundreds of volunteers to be the first to attend. However, Arkansas Governor Orval Faubus stopped the plan. A **federal** court ordered him to obey the law, but the governor ignored the order. In

Members of an angry ▶ mob scream at Central High student Elizabeth Eckford. Eckford was one of nine black students who attended Central High in 1957.

September of 1957, Governor Faubus used the Arkansas **National Guard** to prevent black students from entering the school.

President Dwight D. Eisenhower decided to meet with Governor Faubus. As the head of the **executive branch**, the president is responsible for **enforcing** the law. Eisenhower was angered by the governor's violation of a federal court order. At their meeting, Faubus promised to allow the students to attend the school, and pledged to protect them with the help of the National Guard. However, when Faubus returned to Arkansas, he sent the troops home. As the students entered their new school for the first day, they faced an angry mob of people who screamed at and taunted them. The people were so violent that they beat reporters and smashed many of the school's windows and doors. Local police had to help the students escape.

▲ President Eisenhower (left) and Governor Faubus meet in Newport, Rhode Island, on September 14, 1957.

President Eisenhower decided to send in troops from the U.S. Army's elite 101st Airborne Division to take control of the Arkansas National Guard. For the rest of the school year, students were under the protection of the national government and were able to attend classes.

The crisis at Little Rock Central High School was just one of many tests that the nation would face in the coming years. The president's decision to enforce laws protecting the students was an important moment in the **civil rights** movement. Over the next decade, blacks continued to demand and eventually won their civil rights in the face of mass resistance.

# Introduction to the Executive Branch

**D**uring the spring of 1787, a group of men gathered to make a plan for the United States government. The written document that they created is called the U.S. **Constitution**.

George Washington was ▶ the first president of the United States. This painting shows him being sworn into office on April 30, 1789.

## Fact File

**Head of the Executive Branch**: President of the United States

**Oath of Office**: I do solemnly swear (or affirm) that I will faithfully execute the office of the President of the United States, and will, to the best of my ability, preserve, protect, and defend the Constitution of the United States, so help me God.

**Official Residence**: The White House

**Term of Office**: Four years

**Number of Terms Allowed**: Two

**Election**: Every four years

**Qualifications**: A president must be at least 35 years old and a natural-born citizen of the United States. He or she must also have been a resident of the United States for at least fourteen years.

**Salary**: $400,000 per year

◄ The Constitution is largely based on a plan written by James Madison of Virginia. Many people still look to Madison's notes from the 1787 gathering and his other writings to learn more about the Constitution.

The U.S. Constitution is the law of the land. All parts of the government must abide by the Constitution, including the president of the United States. The Constitution explains how to govern the United States. It also describes how the document can be amended—or changed—as new issues arise that the original authors of the Constitution never imagined.

The Constitution divides the government into three branches, or parts. They are the **legislative branch**, the **judicial branch**, and the executive branch. The legislative branch makes the laws. The judicial branch interprets the laws and makes sure that they agree with the Constitution. The executive branch carries out and enforces the laws.

During the crisis in Little Rock, President Eisenhower remarked that the United States is "a nation in which laws, not men, are supreme." As you have read, the president must sometimes use force to ensure that laws remain supreme. In this book, you will learn more about the duties and powers of the president and the executive branch of the United States government.

# Executive Checks and Balances

The writers of the Constitution knew what could happen if one government body had too much power. Back when the United States was still the Thirteen Colonies, it was ruled by Great Britain. The British government passed laws that affected the colonies without getting any input from the colonists. Since Great Britain was a monarchy, the colonists could not do anything to challenge these laws. They felt powerless.

After the United States gained independence from Great Britain, the drafters of the Constitution worked to limit the power given to the U.S. government. They decided to divide power between the national government and state governments. This is called a **federal system** of government. The drafters then divided the national government into three branches, which created a **separation of powers**. Finally, they worked out a system in which each branch could check, or limit, the powers of the other branches. In this way, a balance of power would exist among the three branches. This is called a system of **checks and balances**.

**Executive Checks and Balances**

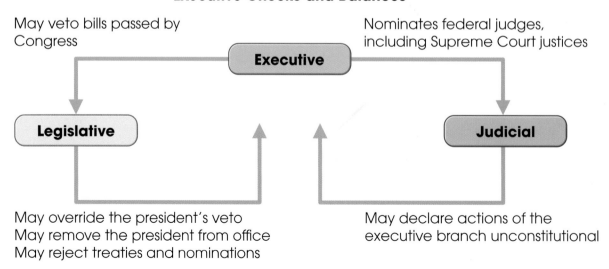

May veto bills passed by Congress

Nominates federal judges, including Supreme Court justices

Executive

Legislative

Judicial

May override the president's veto
May remove the president from office
May reject treaties and nominations

May declare actions of the executive branch unconstitutional

◄ No other president has used the veto power as often as Franklin Delano Roosevelt. During his presidency, Roosevelt vetoed 635 bills. In this photograph, Roosevelt addresses Congress.

## Executive and Judicial Checks

The Constitution gives presidents the power to nominate federal judges, including Supreme Court **justices**. Presidents often try to choose candidates who share their political views.

The judicial branch has a powerful check on the executive branch, too. The Supreme Court can declare actions of the executive branch unconstitutional.

## Executive and Legislative Checks

One of the most powerful checks the Constitution gives the executive branch is the presidential **veto**. When members of the legislative branch want a new law, they create a **bill**, or draft of the law. They then send the bill to the president. The president can either sign the bill, which then becomes a law, or the president can veto (reject) the bill. However, the president does not always make the final decision on a bill. If two-thirds of the members of the House of Representatives and the Senate vote to **override** the president's veto, the bill will then become a law. In this way, the legislative branch has a check on the executive branch.

The legislative branch has another check on the executive branch: the Senate's power to reject **treaties** (written agreements between the United States and foreign countries) and **nominations** made by the president. The Constitution also gives the legislative branch the power to remove a president from office if it **impeaches** and convicts the president of "treason, bribery, or other high crimes and misdemeanors."

Despite the checks on the executive branch, the president still has great influence on the general plans and goals set by the government. In the next chapter, you will read about the president's role in government.

# The Powers of the President

▼ President Gerald Ford announces the pardon of former President Richard Nixon, who resigned in disgrace in 1974. Nixon and others had participated in illegal activities related to the burglary and wiretapping of rival politicians' headquarters.

The main function of the executive branch and the president is to carry out and enforce the law. However, the Constitution gives the president additional responsibilities. Below are just a few of these duties.

## Armed Forces

One of the president's most important duties is defending the United States. The president is the **commander in chief** of the armed forces and has unlimited authority to direct the movements of the U.S. military in order to protect the country. However, the president does not have the power to declare war. The Constitution gives that power to **Congress** (the legislative branch of the United States government).

## Judicial Powers

The president has the authority to nominate **ambassadors** (people who represent the United States in foreign countries), federal judges, and other high-ranking officials. However, these nominations must also be approved by the Senate.

The Constitution also gives the president the judicial power to grant **pardons**. Pardons excuse people who have committed crimes against the United States.

## Leading Legislation

Although the legislative branch creates new laws, the president suggests laws to Congress. Every year, the president gives the "State of the Union Address," a speech in which the president tells Congress how the nation is doing and describes recent accomplishments. The president also describes plans for the coming year and explains programs and **policies** that the president thinks the nation should implement.

As you have read, the president has another important legislative power: the veto. The president can use the veto to reject laws passed by the legislative branch, although Congress can override the veto if two-thirds of both houses vote to do so.

## Relations with Other Countries

The president is responsible for relations with the rest of the world. The president often meets with leaders and representatives from other countries in order to build international friendships and cooperation. The Constitution gives the president authority to make treaties with other nations. However, two-thirds of the Senate must approve each treaty.

As you can see, the president has an enormous amount of responsibility. In the next section, you will learn about other members of the executive branch who help the president carry out executive duties.

▲ President Ronald Reagan (right) and Soviet leader Mikhail Gorbachev sign the INF Treaty in 1987. This was the first treaty to reduce the number of nuclear arms (highly destructive weapons) each country possessed.

# The President's Administration

**M**any people support the president in all aspects of the president's life, such as keeping track of the president's busy schedule and providing information on important issues. This chapter introduces a few of these people and the role they play within a president's **administration**.

## The Vice President

The Constitution does not define the role of the vice president in detail, and the responsibilities of the job have changed through time. Some vice presidents have had close ties to the president, while others have not been involved in making decisions. However, the responsibilities of the vice president have grown. Today, the vice president must be very informed of the president's duties and prepared to become the leader of the country.

The main duty of the vice president is to take control if the president dies or leaves office for any reason. (In 1947, Congress passed an act that listed other officials who will succeed the president if the vice president isn't able to do so.) The vice president is also the leader of the Senate.

## Executive Departments

The **executive departments** are among the most important of the

Robert F. Kennedy (right) was appointed attorney general in 1961 by his brother, President John F. Kennedy (left). After President Kennedy's assassination in 1963, Robert Kennedy continued to serve as attorney general to President Lyndon Johnson before resigning in 1964. ▶

groups that support the president. They are led by people who are experts in their fields and are able to offer the president good advice. The leaders of the executive departments are called **secretaries**.

George Washington, the first president of the United States, asked Congress to approve several executive departments. These included the Department of Foreign Affairs (which later became the State Department), the Department of the Treasury, the War Department (which later became the Department of Defense), and the Department of Justice.

President Washington also started the tradition of regularly meeting with the department secretaries. In 1793, President James Madison began to use the term "**cabinet**" to describe the secretaries as a group. Gradually, as the responsibilities of the executive branch have increased, Congress has created new executive departments.

Today, there are fifteen executive departments. Each department has specific responsibilities. On this page is a chart that describes the four original departments, which are still among the most important today.

Each executive department includes a number of **agencies** that focus on specific tasks. For example, the Department of Justice includes the Drug Enforcement Agency (DEA), which enforces laws relating to illegal drugs, and the Federal Bureau of Investigation (FBI), the federal police force that conducts investigations on behalf of the U.S. government.

**Department of Defense** – Oversees everything related to national security. The secretary of defense directs all armed forces, including the Army, Navy, Air Force, and Marines.

**Department of State** – Handles the U.S. government's relations with the rest of the world. It works with foreign nations on global issues such as terrorism, disease, and the environment. The secretary of state acts on the president's behalf to negotiate treaties with other countries.

**Department of the Treasury** – Manages the financial concerns of the government. It has many agencies, including the Internal Revenue Service (IRS), which collects income taxes.

**Department of Justice** – Responsible for the enforcement of all federal laws. It represents the U.S. government in legal matters and gives legal advice to the president and other members of the cabinet. Unlike the other departments, the head of the Department of Justice is called the attorney general.

# The Executive Office of the President

In addition to the executive departments, the president has the support of offices and agencies within the **Executive Office of the President**. These offices—some of which are listed below—help develop and put into place the policies of the president's administration.

**Council of Economic Advisers** – Creates an economic policy that promotes employment, production, and purchasing power.

**Council on Environmental Quality** – Creates policies that will preserve the environment and the nation's natural resources.

**Office of Management and Budget** – Prepares the federal **budget**.

**National Security Council** – Advises and assists the president on national security and foreign policy.

**Office of the United States Trade Representative** – Develops and coordinates U.S. international trade.

**Domestic Policy Council** – Helps coordinate the policies that affect the nation and works to make sure that they are consistent throughout federal agencies.

Executive Office officials have grown in influence. Some now affect the president's decisions and policies as much or more so than cabinet officials.

There are also many people within the **White House** who support the president and the president's advisers. They include researchers, administrative staff, social secretaries, and others. Among these officials is the White House chief of staff, who keeps track of everything the president needs to know (such as the president's daily schedule), and the **press secretary**, who represents the president to the press and the public.

## Independent Agencies

The members of the cabinet and the Executive Office are the president's main source of information. Together, they make up the president's administration. However, dozens of other federal agencies assist the executive branch in its work. These agencies are responsible for keeping the government and economy running smoothly. They include the Central Intelligence Agency (CIA), the Environmental Protection Agency (EPA), the National Endowment for the Arts (NEA), the Federal Trade Commission (FTC), and the U.S. Postal Service (USPS), among others.

The executive branch is an enormous and powerful part of the government. In the next section, you will read more about how the president and the executive branch influence the decisions of the United States government.

**The President's Administration**

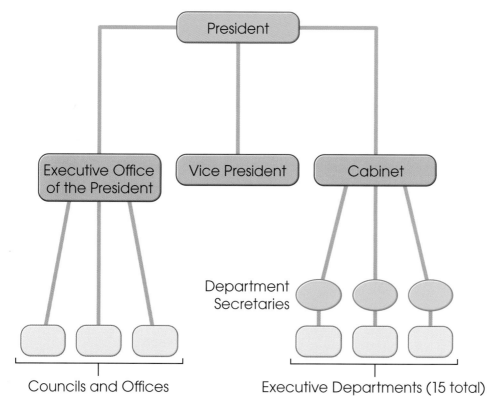

Councils and Offices                    Executive Departments (15 total)

# The President Sets Policies

The president and his administration have a great deal of influence on both the domestic and foreign policies of the United States. Policies are overall plans or general goals pursued by the government. Domestic policies apply to the United States. Foreign policies determine how the United States relates to other nations.

▼ During his two terms in office, President Bill Clinton was known for giving many press conferences. At press conferences, presidents share information about current events that are important to the general public.

Every president comes to office with ideas about what policies the nation should pursue. Most of the time, the president belongs to a **political party**. Political parties are groups that have similar ideas about government and the policies it should pursue. They seek to influence policies by getting their members elected to public office. The two largest political parties in the United States are the Democratic and Republican parties. Every president since 1853 has been either a Democrat or a Republican.

Presidents can influence policy by suggesting bills to Congress. They can also guide policy through the executive departments. Presidents work with their cabinet officers to ensure that the executive departments create programs favored by their administrations.

Presidents also have a powerful tool, called the **executive order**. Presidents give executive orders to the executive departments and federal agencies. These orders are just like laws, except they do not

require the approval of Congress. The president can enforce these orders unless Congress or the courts overturn them.

Another way presidents guide policy is through budget proposals. A budget is a plan for how the government will bring in and spend money. The Constitution does not require the president to make a budget. However, Congress has passed laws that require the president to submit an annual budget. Presidents can use their budget proposals to direct the nation's **resources** toward policies and programs that they favor.

As you can see, the president has a big influence on the policies and activities of the country. In the next section, you will read about how a person can become president.

▲ Presidents have made many important policy changes through executive orders. In 1948, President Harry Truman issued Executive Order 9981, which established equality in treatment and opportunity in the armed services for people of all races. This photograph shows African-American and white soldiers at a base in Italy during World War II.

# Electing a President

Not everyone can be president of the United States. According to the Constitution, presidential **candidates** must be at least 35 years old and born in the United States. The writers of the Constitution included the natural-born citizen qualification because at the time, they were concerned that rulers from other nations might try to control the United States.

The Constitution also explains how the president is to be elected. You may be surprised to learn that the people of the United States do not directly elect their president. The writers of the Constitution wanted to divide power between the national and state governments. They appointed a group of individuals—called electors—from each state to

▼ In 2004, supporters of California Governor Arnold Schwarzenegger, who was born in Austria, introduced a constitutional **amendment** to alter the natural-born citizen qualification. It has not yet passed.

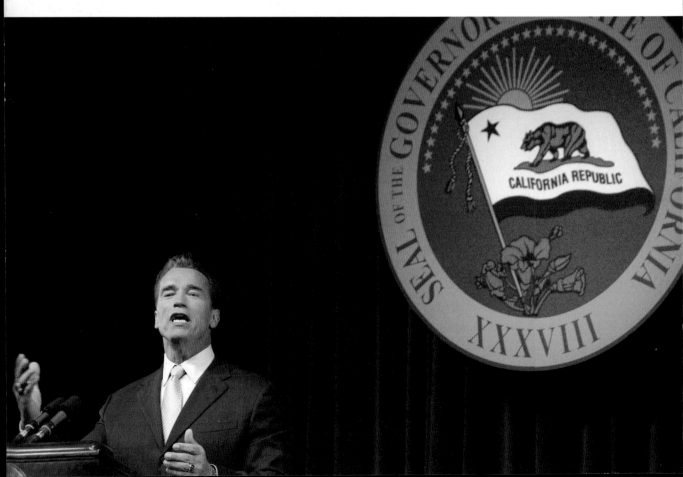

vote for the president and vice president. Together, this group is called the **electoral college**. The number of electors in each state must be equal to the number of **representatives** and senators the state has in Congress. Today, 538 electors make up the electoral college.

Even though the votes of individuals do not directly elect the president, the **popular vote** plays an important role in the outcome of presidential elections. Almost every state awards all of its electoral votes to the winner of the state's popular vote. This is often called a winner-take-all system of elections. Nevertheless, it is possible that the states' electoral votes could produce a different result than the nationwide popular vote. Such an event occurred as recently as 2000. Presidential candidate Al Gore received slightly more popular votes than George W. Bush, but Bush received a majority of electoral votes. As a result, Bush became the 43rd president of the United States.

According to the Constitution, presidential elections occur every four years. The authors of the Constitution placed no limits on how many times an individual could run for the presidency. However, in 1951, the 22nd Amendment limited presidents to just two **terms**.

▲ President Franklin Delano Roosevelt was the only president elected to office four times. The 22nd Amendment limited presidents after Roosevelt to two terms.

# A Day in the Life of the President

During the course of a routine day, the president has to make many important decisions. In order to make wise decisions, the president has numerous meetings with White House staff, members of Congress, and other senior officials.

## Morning

Like most of the nation's representatives, the president begins the day early. The president might eat breakfast with the **first family** in the White House, or head to the **West Wing** for a morning meal. The West Wing of the White House is the location of the executive offices—including the president's **Oval Office**.

After breakfast, the president might meet with the chief of staff to discuss the day's scheduled events, such as speeches or press conferences. Throughout the morning, meetings with senior officials continue. The national security advisor, cabinet secretaries, and officials from the CIA might all have their turn **briefing** the president or asking for the president's decisions on important national questions.

▲ President George W. Bush attends a cabinet meeting in the Cabinet Room of the White House. The cabinet meets around an oval mahogany conference table. Each cabinet member is positioned at the table according to the date his or her department was established.

## Midday

Lunch is often the occasion for more meetings. It is not unusual for a president to have 10 to 20 meetings and to talk with as many as 50 people during a day. Perhaps the luncheon is with a visiting leader. As head of state, it is the president's job to meet with foreign **dignitaries**. The president might use such an occasion to discuss trade or political relations between their two nations. Other times, the president may take a break in the afternoon. President George W. Bush is an avid runner and sometimes goes jogging during the day.

## Evening

The president will often spend evenings hosting or attending important events. One event that might take place is a special bill-signing ceremony. When Congress sends the president an important bill, the president will invite to the signing people who helped create the bill or who will benefit from its provisions.

The president might also leave Washington, D.C., to attend an event. As a national figure, the president makes frequent trips around the country. Late in the afternoon, the president and senior staff might board Air Force One and fly to an important meeting or event outside the **capital**. Air Force One is an airplane modified for the president.

The president of the United States is one of the most important leaders in the world. As you can see, the president is also one of the busiest.

▼ Known as the "flying oval office," Air Force One has 4,000 square feet of floor space. It provides enough room for a dining room, quarters for the president and the president's family, and an office for the president's staff.

# Important Presidents of the 1700s and 1800s

## George Washington (1789-1797)

George Washington was born in Virginia on February 22, 1732. In 1775, when Virginia and the other colonies began to fight the British for their independence, Washington became commander in chief of the colonists' army. By 1783, Great Britain was forced to recognize the colonists' independence.

After the states approved the U.S. Constitution, electors chose Washington as the first president. During his two terms, Washington established traditions and customs, such as cabinet meetings, that presidents still follow today. Despite his popularity, Washington established that a president's power should be limited. After his second term, Washington retired to his home at Mount Vernon. He died there on December 14, 1799. The following year, the U.S. capital moved from Philadelphia to Washington, D.C., which was named in honor of the first president.

▼ Jefferson always feared too much national power. Before his death on July 4, 1826, Jefferson asked that a monument at his grave name him as the author of the Declaration of Independence, the author of the Statute of Virginia for religious freedom, and the father of the University of Virginia. No mention is made of his presidency.

## Thomas Jefferson (1801-1809)

Thomas Jefferson, also a Virginian, was born on April 13, 1743. After the colonies began to fight for their independence from Great Britain, Jefferson drafted the Declaration of Independence, which outlined the colonists' reasons for fighting. In 1801, Jefferson became the third president of the United States and served for two terms. He was almost as influential as Washington in establishing the customs and traditions of the executive branch. Jefferson was in favor of limiting the powers of the national government and championed states' rights. He doubled the size of the United States in 1803 by acquiring the Louisiana Territory from France.

Jefferson died on July 4, 1826. Today, the United States celebrates the Declaration of Independence on the Fourth of July holiday.

## Abraham Lincoln (1861–1865)

Abraham Lincoln was born in Kentucky on February 12, 1809. In 1861, Lincoln was elected the sixteenth president of the United States. Soon after he was elected, the northern and southern states entered into the **Civil War** (1861–1865). Lincoln led the northern states to victory, helping to keep the states from dividing into two countries while also bringing an end to slavery.

During his presidency, Lincoln delivered a number of great speeches—including the Gettysburg Address and his two inaugural addresses—which are still celebrated today. President Lincoln won a second term in 1864, but he was assassinated less than one year later.

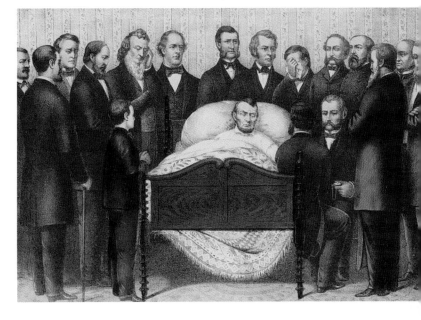

▲ After being shot while attending a performance at Ford's Theatre in Washington, D.C., Lincoln was carried to the Petersen boarding house across the street. His family and government officials waited by his bedside until he died the next morning.

# Important Presidents of the 1900s

### Woodrow Wilson (1913–1921)

Woodrow Wilson was born in Virginia on December 28, 1856. After becoming the 28th president in 1913, Wilson focused on pushing his **reform** policies through Congress. Wilson's reforms led to legislation that created an income tax (a tax on the money you make), and the Federal Reserve System (the central bank of the United States). Wilson also helped establish the Federal Trade Commission, which protects consumers and investigates complaints against companies.

In 1914, World War I began in Europe. Wilson kept the United States out of the war until 1917. After Germany attacked unarmed passenger ships, Wilson asked Congress to declare war and make the world "safe for democracy." The United States helped defeat Germany and its allies. After the war, Wilson assisted in negotiating a peace agreement that included a provision for the League of Nations. This organization was an early form of the United Nations, an international organization of many countries.

▲ President Wilson (far right) meets with European leaders in Paris to set up the Peace Treaty of World War I.

In 1919, Wilson went on tour to drum up popular support for the treaty. Despite his efforts, Wilson failed to win the approval of the Senate, which defeated the treaty in 1920. Wilson passed away four years later, on February 3, 1924.

### Franklin D. Roosevelt (1933–1945)

Franklin Delano Roosevelt was born in New York on January 30, 1882. During his four presidential terms, he led the United States through two of the greatest crises of the 1900s: the Great Depression (1929–1939) and World War II (1939–1945).

Roosevelt began his first term as 32nd president of the United States during the Great Depression, a period of economic hardship and massive unemployment. During his presidency, Roosevelt boldly introduced new programs aimed at reducing economic suffering. In his inaugural address, he told the nation that "the only thing we have to fear is fear itself." Many of Roosevelt's "New Deal" programs are still in place today. Among them is the Social Security system, which gives benefits to workers after they retire.

As president during World War II, Roosevelt served as commander in chief of the armed forces. The United States went to war after an attack on its naval base in Pearl Harbor on December 7, 1941. After Roosevelt's reelection to a fourth term in 1944, U.S. forces and their European allies defeated Nazi Germany and its allies by the spring of 1945. However, Roosevelt served briefly before his death on April 12, 1945.

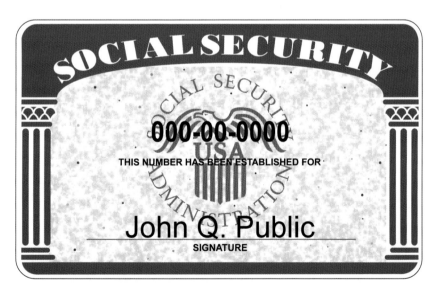

▲ Roosevelt successfully worked with Congress for a Social Security system, which still benefits Americans today. All U.S. citizens are issued a Social Security card with their own personal Social Security number.

# Recent Presidents

### William J. Clinton (1993–2001)

William Jefferson Clinton was born in Arkansas on August 19, 1946. In 1993, Clinton became the 42nd president of the United States and the first Democratic president since Franklin Roosevelt to serve two terms.

During his presidency, Clinton focused on both foreign and domestic policies. In 1994, Clinton won Senate approval for a treaty called NAFTA, which reduced trade barriers between the United States, Canada, and Mexico. Clinton also used his authority to work toward peace in Northern Ireland and troubled areas of Eastern Europe.

Under Clinton, the United States experienced significant economic growth and the first budget **surpluses** in more than 30 years. In addition, both **inflation** and unemployment remained low.

A major disappointment for Clinton was Congress's defeat of his proposal to reform the health care system. Clinton experienced another setback in 1998, when he was impeached over issues related to his relationship with a staff member. However, the Senate found that the President's improper actions were not serious enough to remove him from office.

Today, Clinton continues to be an important figure in American politics. In early 2005, he worked with former President George H. W. Bush to help raise money for the victims of the 2004 tsunami that devastated parts of Asia.

▼ Bill Clinton continues to be active in politics. He often joins former leaders and presidents, such as George H. W. Bush, to attend political events.

George W. Bush ▶ was reelected to a second term as president in 2004. He continues to lead the country through the war on terrorism.

## George W. Bush (2001–2005)

George W. Bush was born in Connecticut on July 6, 1946. In the 2000 election, Bush defeated Al Gore to become the 43rd president of the United States.

On September 11, 2001, during President Bush's first year in office, terrorists attacked the United States, killing thousands. For much of his first term, the president focused his energy on responding to the attacks.

After the attacks, President Bush declared a war on terrorism. The president first dispatched troops to Afghanistan to remove the Taliban regime. The Taliban had provided a safe haven for Osama bin Laden, the leader of Al Qaeda—the group believed to be behind the September 11 attacks.

In March of 2003, the president began a war in Iraq, a country in the Middle East. It was feared that Iraq had obtained weapons of mass destruction. U.S. and British troops quickly removed the regime of Iraq's dictator, Saddam Hussein. Since the fall of Hussein, the United States has had difficulty in maintaining order in Iraq, and weapons of mass destruction have not been found.

Bush won a second term in office in 2004, earning a majority of both the popular and electoral votes. Although conflict continues to erupt in Iraq, the country held its first democratic elections in its history in early 2005, with support from Bush and the U.S. government.

# All About the White House

It may surprise you to learn that Washington, D.C. was not always the nation's capital. The government first met in New York City and then Philadelphia. Only in 1800 did the capital move permanently to Washington, D.C. In November of 1800, John Adams became the first president to live in the White House, the official residence of the president.

The White House was designed by Irish-American architect James Hoban. Hoban is said to have modeled the residence on mansions he was familiar with in Ireland. Since then, the White House has undergone many changes. The British burned the building during the War of 1812. But workers, directed by Hoban, soon rebuilt the White House using the original plans. In the 1820s, Hoban added other features, including terraces and new porticoes (porches) at both the north and south entrances.

▲ This is a partial view of the Oval Office of the White House.

Few other major changes were made to the exterior until the presidency of Theodore Roosevelt (1901–1909). In 1902, Roosevelt ordered the construction of a new West Wing to house the executive offices, including the president's oval office. An East Wing, built in 1942, added even more space.

The interior of the White House has also undergone changes through the years. Many changes were minor, with each president remodeling according to his family's tastes. At times, however, more significant alterations were needed. During the presidency of Harry Truman (1945–1953), engineers found that the building's structure had weakened. Between 1948 and 1952, workers gutted the interior of the White House and replaced the wood structure with concrete and steel.

Today, the White House boasts more than 100 rooms, including a movie theater and a bowling alley. The main building has a number of large rooms on the first floor that the president uses for receptions and other formal occasions. The second floor serves as the private residence of the president and the first family. Guest rooms and staff quarters occupy much of the third floor.

Many changes have been made to the White House since 1800. Even so, the White House has kept its overall shape for more than two centuries. Over time, the building has come to symbolize the presidency and its importance in the United States and around the world.

▼ People began calling the president's mansion the "White House" shortly after it was built because the mansion's white-gray sandstone contrasted with the red brick of nearby buildings. However, it did not become the official name of the building until 1902.

# Glossary

**administration**  group consisting of the president, the president's cabinet, and the Executive Office of the President

**agency**  establishment engaged in doing business for another group

**ambassador**  messenger or representative

**amendment**  change or addition to the Constitution

**bill**  early version or draft of a law

**briefing**  meeting at which officials give important information

**budget**  plan for raising and spending money

**cabinet**  group made up of the heads of the executive departments; it advises the president

**candidate**  individual who has qualified and is running for office

**capital**  city that serves as the seat of government

**checks and balances**  system that makes sure a branch of government does not become stronger than another branch

**civil rights**  rights of citizens, especially those given by the 13th and 14th Amendments to the Constitution that guarantee equal protection of the laws and freedom from discrimination

**Civil War (1861–1865)**  war between the U.S. government and 11 Southern states that fought to withdraw from the Union

**commander in chief**  president of the United States in the role of leader of the armed forces

**Congress**  legislative branch of the United States; it has two houses: the Senate and the House of Representatives

**constitution**  document containing a country's basic principles and laws, which describe the powers and duties of the government

**dignitary**  individual who holds high rank or a position of honor

**electoral college**  group of electors appointed by the states to vote for the president and vice president

**enforcing**  causing obedience to a law, regulation, or command

**executive branch**  part of the government that carries out and enforces laws

**executive department**  one of the departments in the executive branch that assists the president in overseeing and carrying out national policy

**Executive Office of the President**  group of the president's immediate staff that helps develop and implement the policy and programs of the president

**executive order**  order the president gives to an executive department or federal agency; it has the effect of law

**federal**  of or relating to the national government as distinct from the state governments

**federal system**  system in which power is divided between a national and state governments

**first family**  president's family

**impeach**  charge a public official with misconduct in public office

**inflation**  rise in the general price of things; inflation occurs when there is more money circulating than there are available products to buy

**integrate**  make a group, community, place, or organization and its opportunities available to all people of different races or ethnic groups

**judicial branch**  part of the government that interprets the law

**justice**  judge of the Supreme Court

**legislative branch**  part of the government that makes laws

**National Guard**  military force organized by each state and equipped by the federal government

**nomination**  proposal of a candidate for election of office

**Oval Office**  president's office in the West Wing of the White House

**override**  cancel or change an action taken by somebody else

**pardon**  power of the president to forgive individuals for offenses

**policy**  program of actions put into practice by a government

**political party**  group of people who have similar views about government

**popular vote**  vote of the public

**press secretary**  official who represents the president to the media and the public

**reform**  change for the better, improve

**representative**  individual elected by citizens to represent them in government

**resources**  natural supply of wealth or revenue

**secretary**  leader of a department in the executive branch of the U.S. government

**segregation**  isolation of a group of people brought about by forcing its members to live in certain areas or by preventing its members from using facilities used by other groups

**separation of powers**  system of government that distributes power among several branches

**Supreme Court**  highest federal court in the United States

**surplus**  money left over after all costs have been paid

**term**  length of time, set by law, served by an elected official

**treaty**  formal contract or agreement between two countries

**unconstitutional**  in disagreement with the principles or laws in the Constitution

**veto**  power of the president to reject bills passed by Congress

**West Wing**  1902 addition to the White House where the executive offices, including the president's Oval Office, are located

**White House**  official residence of the president

# Further Reading

Giesecke, Ernestine. *National Government*. Chicago: Heinemann Library, 2000.

Grace, Catherine O'Neill. *The White House: An Illustrated History*. New York: Scholastic, 2003.

Meltzer, Milton. *George Washington and the Birth of Our Nation*. New York: Franklin Watts, 1986.

# Index